21st Century Skills Library

REAL WORLD MATH: HEALTH AND WELLNESS

EXERCISE BY THE NUMBERS

Cecilia Minden

Cherry Lake Publishing
Ann Arbor, Michigan

Published in the United States of America by Cherry Lake Publishing
Ann Arbor, MI
www.cherrylakepublishing.com

Math Adviser: Tonya Walker, MA, Boston University

Nutrition Adviser: Steven Abrams, MD, Professor of Pediatrics, Baylor College of
Medicine, Houston, Texas

Photo Credits: Page 4, © Roy Morsch/Corbis; page 22, Illustration courtesy of U.S.
Department of Agriculture

Library of Congress Cataloging-in-Publication Data
Minden, Cecilia.
  Exercise by the numbers / by Cecilia Minden.
    p. cm. — (Real world math)
  Includes index.
  ISBN-13: 978-1-60279-010-0
  ISBN-10: 1-60279-010-8
  1. Mathematics—Juvenile literature. 2. Exercise—Juvenile literature. 3. Health—Juvenile
literature. I. Title.
  QA40.5.M48 2008
  510—dc22   2007005155

*Cherry Lake Publishing would like to acknowledge the work of
The Partnership for 21st Century Skills.
Please visit www.21stcenturyskills.org for more information.*

TABLE OF CONTENTS

CHAPTER ONE

BREAKING A SWEAT

Playing basketball is a great way to get some exercise.

Y ou and your friends decide to play a game of basketball after school.

You change into shorts and a T-shirt because you know you're probably

going to work up a sweat running, jumping, and shooting the ball. Sure enough, you get a great workout on the court. Your heart is pounding, and you feel is energized. Who would have guessed that exercise could be so much fun?

Have you ever heard the expression "Your body is a machine"? Each organ and cell does its part to make sure your heart is pumping and your muscles are working. To keep a machine running, however, you need to use it on a regular basis. To keep your body running, you need to exercise.

Your heart is one of the most important organs in your body. It has countless functions, such as pumping blood to other major organs. It is also one of the most powerful muscles in your body. Muscles require exercise to stay healthy and strong. When you push yourself to remain in motion for a consistent block of time, you are strengthening all your muscles, including your heart.

There are several other physical and emotional benefits to exercise, including burning calories. The calories you consume when you eat food create energy in your body. In turn, your body uses that energy to work properly. A healthy intake of calories and regular exercise are important parts of a healthy lifestyle.

Too many calories and not enough exercise can lead to trouble. Your body stores unused calories as extra fat. In other words, you gain weight. Being overweight can cause physical problems that may harm your health. Regular exercise is important for burning off those extra calories and keeping your weight at a healthy level. Another advantage to exercise is that it improves

how you feel. Physical changes occur when you experience stress. Exercise

relieves some of this stress. Taking a brisk walk or a quick swim can help

*Yoga is a great way to increase your flexibility and calm your mind. Your
doctor can help you learn more about whether yoga is right for you.*

you calm down. Whatever form of exercise you choose, staying physically active not only relieves stress and lifts your spirits. It can also help you feel more energetic and provide you with a sense of accomplishment.

Now you know the benefits of exercise. Are you ready to run that machine of yours? Math skills and your knowledge of nutrition will help you get your body in the best possible shape.

REAL WORLD MATH CHALLENGE

Rosa is feeling tense about the upcoming school spelling bee. She has 2 hours and 45 minutes before the bee begins. She wants to spend at least 30 minutes going over some tough words. She needs about 20 minutes to change into a new outfit. It will take her approximately 10 minutes to get to her school. **Does Rosa have any time left to exercise? If the answer is yes, what percentage of her time before the bee can she devote to exercising?**

(Turn to page 29 for the answers)

Many people enjoy swimming because it is great exercise
and can help you keep cool when it is hot outside.

WORKING OUT THE WAY YOU WANT

You get out of bed one Saturday morning and want to start your day off

with a little exercise. Should you ride your bike or meet your friends for a

game of soccer at the park? Raking the leaves seems less fun, but you know

Raking leaves is one chore that can give you a good workout.

it's on your list of chores and is still a form of exercise. How will you get

your daily workout?

Team sports are one option. Working together with other people to

achieve a common goal has many rewards. Being on a team gives you the

opportunity to learn about cooperation and respect and to improve your

self-confidence. Kids who play on teams say they like belonging to a group.

They know they have the support of their teammates. Whether they win or

lose, they are spending time with their friends while staying in shape.

REAL WORLD MATH CHALLENGE

Sean and 13 of his friends decide to play a game of dodgeball. Counting Sean, there are 8 boys and 6 girls. Everyone agrees that there should be as even a mix as possible of both boys and girls on each of two teams. **How many players should each team have? On each of the teams, how many players should be girls? How many should be boys? What percentage of the players in the game are girls? What percentage are boys?**

(Turn to page 29 for the answers)

Do you like to work with other people to accomplish goals? Then team sports might be for you. Baseball, football, hockey, soccer, and basketball are well-known team sports, but there are many others to choose from. In Ultimate Frisbee, two teams of seven players try to score points by throwing and catching the Frisbee on opposite ends of the field. Other sports such as gymnastics and track take turns focusing on individual team members. There are team sports that fit all athletic skills and preferences. Explore your options. Decide which one is right for you.

On the other hand, there are also benefits to exercising on your own or doing an activity that doesn't involve teams. You can take private or group classes such as ballet or gymnastics. Skateboarding, and running are also fun options. You learn self-discipline as you push yourself to become better and better over time. It is rewarding to set and achieve personal goals.

Household chores or yard work may not be as appealing as the different types of exercise discussed so far. They do, however, offer a convenient opportunity to burn some calories. You can get creative, too! Shoveling snow with your sister is also

Hiking is fun and a great way to enjoy the outdoors.

the perfect setting for a snowball fight. Sweeping or mopping might even

be fun if you have your MP3 player handy.

CHAPTER THREE

DO THE MATH: PACE YOURSELF

When you exercise, you need to be sure you are working your body hard enough, but not pushing yourself too hard.

You need to use a machine regularly to keep it running. If you use it too long or too often, however, your machine might break down. You need to be careful not to overdo physical activity. This is particularly important when you're starting a new workout routine. How can you figure out if you are doing a good job of pacing yourself?

Determining your *target* heart rate provides useful information to answer this question. This is the rate at which your heart should beat during exercise without being overworked. Once you've reached your target heart rate, you're at a point where you are gaining the greatest amount of physical benefits from your workout routine. A gym teacher or sports coach can help you calculate this figure.

First, however, you need to *predict* your maximum heart rate. This is the fastest your heart should beat when exercising or doing some form of physical activity. You can determine this rate by subtracting your age from the number *220*. If you are 11, your predicted maximum heart rate would be 209 (220 − 11) beats per minute.

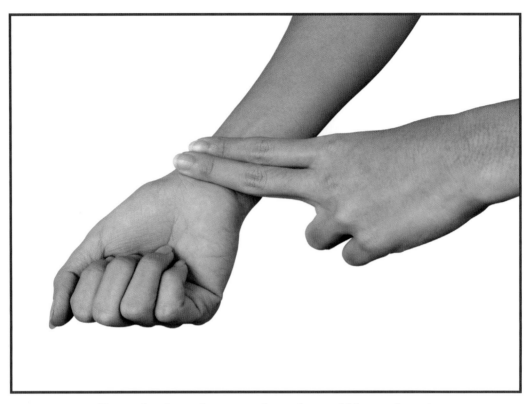

You need to determine your pulse, or how quickly your heart is beating, to find out if you are reaching your target heart rate.

Your target heart rate should be between 60 percent and 80 percent of

your predicted maximum heart rate. For an 11-year-old, target heart rate

should be between 125 (209 x .6) and 167 (209 x .8) beats per minute.

You can figure out if you're at your target heart rate by measuring your pulse rate after you exercise. Your pulse rate is the number of times your heart beats in 1 minute. You can have someone take your pulse for an entire minute. You can also take the number of beats after 10 seconds and multiply by 6 (since there are 60 seconds in 1 minute).

Is the number you come up with beneath the range of your target heart rate? Then gradually increase the amount of time and the difficulty level of your exercise. Is the number you calculate above the range of your target heart rate? You may be overdoing it. Consider taking time out to rest or reducing the amount of physical activity involved in your routine.

REAL WORLD MATH CHALLENGE

Joshua is 12. His gym teacher takes his pulse after he exercises and counts 16 beats in 10 seconds. **What is Joshua's pulse? What is his target heart rate? How does his heart rate after exercising compare to his target heart rate?**

(Turn to page 29 for the answers)

Your target heart rate is just one indicator of how well you are pacing yourself. You know your body better than anyone else. It will give you the best clues about whether you can push yourself harder or need to take a break. It is time to stop if you are having difficulty

You can use a notebook or calendar to keep track of the intensity of your workouts.

breathing, feel dizzy, are extremely tired, or begin experiencing cramps.

You may want to kick up your level of physical activity a if your heart isn't

beating faster than normal.

You can use a journal or calendar to record the intensity of your workouts. Don't forget to occasionally note how much closer you are to reaching your target heart rate. At first, your machine might need a little tune-up. It won't be long before you have it running smoothly again if you increase your physical activity. Use your math skills to help you achieve your exercise goals.

REAL WORLD MATH CHALLENGE

One Friday, Kim decides she wants to get some exercise, but there are no formal sports activities going on after school. Luckily, Kim is creative and still manages to get in some exercise. She walks home, which takes about 14 minutes. Then she spends about 25 minutes raking leaves. Next, she plays Frisbee for 30 minutes with her friends. Then she takes the dog on a 15-minute walk. **Did Kim exercise more than an hour? If so, by how much?**

(Turn to page 29 for the answers)

CHAPTER FOUR

DO THE MATH:
FEEL THE BURN!

It's noon, and you're starving. You've just finished a game of softball. You

know that later on your mom needs some help cleaning the house. You

want to eat a meal that fills you up and gives you energy for the chores you

A healthy lifestyle includes rest and quiet activities,
such as reading, along with plenty of exercise.

have to do later. How many calories should you take in? How can you be sure to burn them off later?

Most 10- to 12-year-olds of average size need about 2,000 calories a day, depending on how active they are. Someone involved in sports or who exercises often burns more calories than someone who is less physically active. When you eat more calories than your body uses in a day, your body stores the extra energy as fat, and you gain weight.

You're more likely to keep your calorie count in the right range for you by including a healthy balance of foods from all the different groups listed at www.MyPyramid.gov. The food pyramid places foods in the following categories: grains, vegetables, fruits, milk, meat and beans, and oils.

Grains are foods made from wheat, rice, oats, barley, and other whole grains. Vegetables can be fresh, frozen, canned, or dried. Whole fruits or

Each color on the food pyramid represents a different food group. Visit www.MyPyramid.gov to find out more about the food groups and healthy eating.

100 percent fruit juice are a part of the fruit group. Milk and products

made from milk, such as yogurt and cheese, are in the milk group. Foods in the meat and bean group include meat (beef and pork, for example), poultry, fish, nuts, eggs, and beans (including black, kidney, and navy beans). The oils category features liquid oils such as olive and canola oil, solid fats such as butter, and other foods high in fat content such as mayonnaise and salad dressings. The Web site also includes information on serving sizes and how many servings you need from each food group every day.

There's no doubt that exercise burns calories. Different physical activities perform this function at different rates. Math skills and an understanding of balanced nutrition and various forms of exercise

21st Century Content

Balancing the number of calories you take in each day with the number of calories you burn is an important part of staying healthy. If you want to get an idea of how many calories you will burn doing a certain activity, try visiting a Web site such as Calorie Control.org (www. caloriecontrol.org/ exercalc.html). This site lets you input your weight and the length of time you plan to do an activity. Then it tells you how many calories you can expect to burn.

will help you make good choices. You can decide the best ways for you

to balance the number of calories you eat with your level of activity. You

don't want to load your machine (your body) with extra fuel to make it

run and then not put it to good use.

REAL WORLD MATH CHALLENGE

Nick's regular lunch at the deli includes a sandwich (370 calories), chili (220 calories), and a glass of 2 percent milk (120 calories). Today, he takes advantage of a meal special at a local fast-food restaurant for only $1.00 more. This meal includes a cheeseburger (490 calories), fries (540 calories), and soda (280 calories). Nick can burn about 300 calories an hour playing football. **What is the difference in calories between what Nick normally eats for lunch and what he eats today? How many hours will it take him to burn off the calories he consumes during lunch today? How many hours does it normally take him to burn off the calories he consumes during lunch?**

(Turn to page 29 for the answers)

CHAPTER FIVE

FIT FOR LIFE

Exercise is a necessary part of a healthy lifestyle. It can be difficult to regularly make time for exercise, but you simply can't do without it. How can you make exercise fit into your schedule? The easiest way is to keep moving.

Do you enjoy running? If you do, make going for a run part of your fitness plan.

*Walking to school with a friend is a great way
to fit exercise into your schedule.*

Do you live close enough to your school that you can walk there? If so,

arrange for your friends to walk with you. If your school features outdoor

recess, use that time to get your heart pumping! Even a short game of tag

can serve as an excellent form of exercise.

What about when you are at home and want to be with your family?

Many families often find themselves watching television together. This activity is okay once in a while, but there is evidence that children who spend a lot of time in front of the television each day have a higher rate of obesity.

Does this mean that television is bad for you? Not at all! But watching hour upon hour of television and not exercising is. Make time with your family valuable by going for a bike ride together or—if you are determined to be in front of the television—exercising to a workout DVD.

REAL WORLD MATH CHALLENGE

Athena decides it's time for her family to do more exercise as a group. She notes that they spend 2.5 hours each night watching television together and only 1.5 hours every Saturday going for a walk or taking a swim in the backyard pool. **How many hours each week does her family spend in front of the television? If they spend 1 less hour watching television each night and use that time to work out, how much exercise will they get in 1 week?**

(Turn to page 29 for the answers)

Your body is the most important machine you will ever care for or operate. You need to keep it in excellent working condition so that it can run efficiently every hour of every day for the rest of your life. Exercise, a healthy diet, and a positive attitude are tools that allow you to do this. Your math skills also come in handy. So, flip the "on" switch. What kind of exercise do you want to try today?

*Working out with your family or friends can
make exercise even more enjoyable!*

REAL WORLD MATH CHALLENGE ANSWERS

Chapter One

Page 9

Keep in mind that there are 60 minutes in 1 hour. Rosa therefore has exactly 165 minutes before the bee begins.

$60 \times 2 = 120$

$120 + 45 = 165$

Of that time, she needs to devote 60 minutes to other activities besides exercise.

$30 \text{ minutes} + 20 \text{ minutes} + 10 \text{ minutes} = 60$

This means she has 105 minutes left over, so she does have time to exercise.

$165 \text{ minutes} - 60 \text{ minutes} = 105 \text{ minutes}$

The time she has to exercise represents 64 percent of her time before the bee.

$105 \div 165 = 0.636 = 64\%$

Chapter Two

Page 11

To play the game fairly, Sean and his friends should have 7 players on each of two teams.

$8 + 6 = 14$

$14 \div 2 = 7$

To make sure each team has an even mix of boys and girls, each side should have 3 girls and 4 boys.

$6 \div 2 = 3 \text{ girls}$

$8 \div 2 = 4 \text{ boys}$

Girls represent 43 percent of the total players in the game, and boys represent 57 percent of the players.

$6 \div 14 = 0.43 = 43\%$

$8 \div 14 = 0.57 = 57\%$

Chapter Three

Page 17

Joshua's pulse is the number of times his heart beats in 1 minute, or 60 seconds. His pulse would therefore be 96 beats per minute.

$6 \times 16 = 96$

To determine his target heart rate, he must first calculate his predicted maximum heart rate, which is 208 beats per minute.

$220 - 12 = 208$

His target heart rate should fall anywhere between 60 percent and 80 percent of this figure, so it would be between 125 and 166 beats per minute.

$208 \times 0.6 = 125$

$208 \times 0.8 = 166$

Joshua's heart rate after exercising is 29 beats per minute less than the lowest number in the range of his target heart rate.

$125 - 96 = 29$

Page 19

Kim spends 84 minutes exercising.

$14 \text{ minutes} + 25 \text{ minutes} + 30 \text{ minutes} + 15 \text{ minutes} = 84 \text{ minutes}$

Since there are 60 minutes in 1 hour, she exercises longer than 1 hour by 24 minutes.

$84 \text{ minutes} - 60 \text{ minutes} = 24 \text{ minutes}$

Chapter Four

Page 24

Nick normally takes in 710 calories during lunch.

$370 \text{ calories} + 220 \text{ calories} + 120 \text{ calories} = 710 \text{ calories}$

Today, he consumes 1,310 calories.

$490 \text{ calories} + 540 \text{ calories} + 280 \text{ calories} = 1,310 \text{ calories}$

This is a difference of 600 calories.

$1,310 \text{ calories} - 710 \text{ calories} = 600 \text{ calories}$

He would have to play football for 4.4 hours to burn off the calories he consumes today at lunch.

$1,310 \div 300 = 4.4$

Normally, it only takes 2.4 hours of playing football to burn off the calories he consumes during lunch.

$710 \div 300 = 2.4$

Chapter Five

Page 27

Athena's family spends 17.5 hours each week watching television together.

$2.5 \times 7 = 17.5$

This is 16 hours more than they spend exercising as a group.

$17.5 - 1.5 = 16$

If they spend 1 less hour each night watching television and instead use that time to exercise, they'll devote a total of 8.5 hours each week to working out as a family.

$1 \times 7 = 7$

$7 + 1.5 = 8.5$

GLOSSARY

calories (KAL-uh-reez) the measurement of the amount of energy available to your body in the food you eat

consume (kuhn-SOOM) to take in

obesity (oh-BEE-suh-tee) the state of being overweight

organs (OR-guhnz) groups of tissues such as the heart, lungs, stomach, or kidneys that perform a specific job within the body

poultry (POHL-tree) birds that are raised for their meat and eggs; chickens, turkeys, ducks, and geese are poultry

yoga (YO-guh) exercise techniques that involve deep breathing and stretching and that are designed to improve both physical and mental well-being

FOR MORE INFORMATION

Books

Goodger, Beverley. *Exercise*. North Mankato, MN: Smart Apple Media, 2005.

Gray, Shirley W. *Exercising for Good Health*.
Chanhassen, MN: The Child's World, 2004.

Wenig, Marsha, and Susan Andrews (photographer). *YogaKids: Educating the Whole Child through Yoga*. New York: Stewart, Tabori & Chang, 2003.

Web Sites

American Heart Association—Children and Exercise
www.americanheart.org/presenter.jhtml?identifier=3007589
For links to information about kids and exercise

U.S. Department of Agriculture—MyPyramid.gov
www.mypyramid.gov/
To learn more about the food groups, healthy eating, and exercise

INDEX

ABOUT THE AUTHOR

Cecilia Minden, PhD, is a literacy consultant and the author of many books for children. She is the former director of the Language and Literacy Program at Harvard Graduate School of Education in Cambridge, Massachusetts. She would like to thank fifth-grade math teacher Beth Rottinghaus for her help with the Real World Math Challenge problems. Cecilia lives with her family in North Carolina.